ANTHONY BOURDAIN
UNLOADED
THE UNCOMMON WISDOM OF A LEGENDARY PROVOCATEUR
JULIANA SHARAF

AN ENTHUSIAST FOR THE AGES

N O ONE GAVE me more hope for the future than the lanky man on my television set striding through a sea of food stalls. It was 2006 and I, a jaded teenager stuck in a virulently conservative suburban hellscape whose culinary offerings were more of the golden arch variety, had just stumbled upon a program unlike any I'd ever encountered. "It's takoyaki time—Osaka style!" he announced, sitting down at a restaurant that specialized in fried octopus dumplings and inviting viewers to gawk at its "disturbingly surrealist window display" of a chopstick-wielding octopus stabbing at baby octopus dumplings. "I'm gonna have nightmares about that guy," he noted. I'd scarcely gotten my bearings before he cut to the chase: "Thankfully, watching plastic octopi devouring their young—while perhaps a moral gray area—does not impact my appetite."

What *was* this show? Who was this salt-and-pepper-haired man with a shit-eating grin reveling in pointing out the absurd without a trace of irony or condescension? This was a far cry from anything squeaky-clean, Disney-shilling fellow Travel Channel host Samantha Brown had ever done, even though she'd logged similar mileage. It was also light-years away from the food shows I grew up with—rather than working in a studio kitchen à la Rachael Ray or Emeril Lagasse (and sans annoying catchphrase), this was a chef taking viewers into the field and onto the front lines of culinary progress, a war correspondent of sorts whose sole purpose was to cut through commercialized bullshit to shine a light on (for all intents and purposes) normal people making recipes handed down to them over generations, eating working-class meals, regional staples and so on. I'd discovered a prophet who delighted in showing me tastier worlds to come if I could just get away from this backwater town mired in a culture of fast food and mediocrity. With that episode of *No Reservations*, the scales had fallen from my eyes. I'd never look at food the same way again. (Sadly, I have not yet acquired a taste for octopus.)

I launched myself full tilt down the rabbit hole of everything Bourdain. As I tore through the pages of his signature work, *Kitchen Confidential*, his eloquent, irreverent writer's voice emblazoning itself on my brain, the city limits of my hometown relinquished their grip on my psyche (I wasn't old enough to drive yet, making this particular brand of escapism all the more necessary). The guy might as well have been a rock star, having come of age in the gritty New York City of the 1970s and '80s, an era of neon-lit sex shops lining Times Square, Guardian Angels standing sentinel in subway cars and other seedy visuals I'd only visited in the form of Steely Dan lyrics or while watching *The Warriors*. Not only had he kicked a heroin habit cold turkey and lived to tell the tale, but he weathered many punishing years satisfying the boozy brunch crowd at venues like the Rainbow Room to then pen a book exposing the unsavory secrets of the restaurant industry, rocketing to stardom at the ripened age of 43. And aside from his witty jokes and penchant for pop culture references, he wrote about the preparation of food with attention, care and an unfaltering self-confidence—a conviction that there was, in fact, a "best" way of doing something, even an act as seemingly mundane as eating an oyster and that you owed it to yourself to savor the simple ritual of that moment rather than cram the thing down your gaping maw without another thought. Here was someone I could trust to tell me the truth about how the world worked—not only that, but how it *could* work—a trust he never betrayed.

In Anthony Bourdain, I discovered a guide and mentor, someone who, in the pursuit of knowledge, gave not one single damn about making an ass of himself. He never attempted to pull the wool over anyone's eyes, as is common among middle-aged men trying to look cool. (For an early example of this, check out the second episode of *No Reservations*, all too appropriately titled "Iceland: Hello Darkness My Old Friend," in which our hero spends the majority of the program cursing and freezing his ass off in blue jeans amid the bleak icy tundra, the picture of misery.) Bourdain's love of occupying the lowest rung on any given hierarchy of skill, his all-eclipsing willingness to humble himself time and again, appealed to me in its total lack of irony. Whenever he walked into someone's grandmother's house to partake in a home-cooked meal (one she'd likely learned to cook from her own grandmother), whether it was in the Tuscan countryside or a rice paddy in Vietnam, the joy that spread over his face while embracing his wizened hostess was palpable.

The 2006 Beirut episode of *No Reservations*, in which he and his crew witness the outbreak of war in Lebanon, marked a turning point: Although he'd been making quality programming since his first show, *A Cook's Tour*, premiered in 2002, Bourdain became aware of his responsibility to document stories borne out of global conflict, the intersection of political maneuvering and human suffering. Following his evacuation out of the country, he returned home and promptly fathered his only child, Ariane. These two events changed his worldview forever, catalyzing moments that put a great deal of things into perspective in a blink.

Where other celebrity chefs sold out or lost sight of their roots while ascending their ivory towers, Tony, as he was known to those who loved him most, did neither. Even as his empire expanded to include numerous Emmys and judge spots on cooking competition shows such as *The Taste* and *Top Chef*, he stayed true to a singular focus: amplifying the voices of the people who prepare the food we eat, from farm to table, never missing an opportunity to highlight the contributions of immigrants to American restaurant culture over the course of his travels. (He somehow also found time outside of filming his CNN series, *Parts Unknown*, to maintain a well-written Tumblr blog, author a graphic novel, lend his voice to a disgruntled chef on *Archer* and regularly lambaste Donald Trump on Twitter, among other projects. Did he ever sleep?) Ever the pragmatist, he summed himself up in one word, memorialized in his Twitter bio: "Enthusiast." And then, one summer day in 2018, for reasons he did not share, he ended it all. No one has come close to filling the void left in his wake.

While this is by no means an attempt to recount every lesson that can be gleaned from his fruitful career, I hope this compendium of Bourdainian brilliance inspires you to broaden your perspective and gain a greater understanding of how food does more than nourish: It connects us with the land on which we live and, more importantly, with each other. Bourdain's unique insights widened my horizon when I needed it most. All there is to do, he'd say, is get up off your couch and move.

—Juliana Sharaf

On a book tour
in China, 2005.

"At their best, chefs like to consider themselves alchemists, and some of them, particularly the French, have a long and glorious tradition of turning lead into gold."

—*A Cook's Tour: Global Adventures in Extreme Cuisines*

Cultural staples aren't just culinary reflections of local flora and fauna. Frequently, such dishes are an edible legacy, the tasty results of desperate people from generations past who discovered how to get the most out of every part of an animal—even the unspeakable bits—in a triumph over starvation, waste and going broke. If a peasant with inconsistent access to clean drinking water can make a seminal dish out of snails or frog legs, you can figure out how to get the most out of that head of lettuce that's been hanging out in your icebox all week.

"It was never useful to me to think about what people like or don't like."

—*Bon Appétit*, 2016

TRUST YOUR GUT

NOT MANY PEOPLE could say with a straight face that they'd be thrilled to make a living dunking french fries while staring down the barrel of middle age. Anthony Bourdain certainly wasn't. By 43, the executive chef at Brasserie Les Halles had led a colorful, low-key life: He'd graduated from the Culinary Institute of America, married his high school sweetheart, worked his way through a number of New York restaurants and kicked a heroin habit cold turkey. He'd also amassed quite a bit of debt and couldn't, one imagines, shake the specter of a question that lingers in the mind of anyone who works a physically and emotionally exhausting job: *How much longer can I keep this up?*

It's a difficult business tracing the trajectory of a life and boiling it down to a series of choices, often because there's no telling where the roads you take (e.g., "It's 5 a.m.: Should

I write or go back to bed?") will lead. Bourdain couldn't have imagined *Kitchen Confidential: Adventures in the Culinary Underbelly*, his 2000 ode to restaurant life, would lead to a career traveling to far-flung reaches of the globe. All he knew was that he wanted to write, and if he was going to do that, it'd have to be at the crack of dawn before his culinary duties beckoned him back to the kitchen.

But *Kitchen Confidential* was hardly Bourdain's first foray into writing. He'd taken the old adage "write what you know" to heart by penning an autobiographical short story about a chef scoring heroin on the Lower East Side. This early work (the title has since been lost to time) got picked up in *Between C & D*, a Lower East Side alternative literary magazine. And where most might be content to savor a fleeting glimmer of fame before going about their lives, Bourdain was keen to keep up the momentum. Ever the masochist, he headed uptown to Columbia University to sit in at a writing workshop led by Gordon Lish. A fiction editor at Knopf (and formerly *Esquire*), Lish had savaged the works of Vladimir Nabokov, Raymond Carver and a slew of authors in service of the written word. He was a prickly presence whose mantra, "Seduce the whole fucking world for all time," continues to shock and awe. Bourdain was drawn like a moth to the flame.

Was it fun to read his work aloud and be cut off by

Lish and dogpiled on by classmates? Hardly. But it proved transformative.

In a 2016 interview with *Bon Appétit*, Bourdain shared the ethos that drove his literary output: "It was never useful to me to think about what people like or don't like. When I wrote *Kitchen Confidential*, I expected no one to read it and that was really a liberating place to be. I've stuck with that model since."

Daring to envision a different life for yourself need not look like assembling a mood board and manifesting a meeting in a Vietnamese noodle shop with then-president Barack Obama (though, if you were so inclined, it couldn't hurt). All too often, it begins by asking what you could do differently—or, if you want to be honest with yourself, doing the thing that makes you the most uncomfortable.

Whether you've been wanting to take a writing workshop like Bourdain did, pick up a new craft or do something as simple as bite into a dirty water hot dog, chase what haunts you regardless (or perhaps in spite of) what others might think.

When it comes to dishes that linger in your memory long after the last morsel has dissolved on your tongue, remember: Price is no guarantee of quality. More importantly for Bourdain, excellent meals were the alchemical result of abandoning any notion of pretense, reveling in the camaraderie of good company and allowing yourself to delight in the (more often than not humble) circumstances that led you to the table, booth or cart on the street.

"I was a happy dishwasher. I jokingly say that I learned every important lesson, all the most important lessons of my life as a dishwasher."

—NPR's *Fresh Air*, 2016

EVERY MASTER IS A STUDENT

THERE'S ONE SIMPLE if morbid question that chefs are particularly fond of asking each other: What would you eat for your last meal? Also known as the "death row meal," it's as much a peek into the psyche of every great cook as it is a profile of one's palate. Bourdain's answer changed over the years: In 2009, it was the roasted bone marrow and parsley salad at London's St. John, an unctuous, macabre feast requiring the scraping of actual bones in search of the umami bomb of jellied fat within. But by 2016, a new and lasting favorite had emerged—"a 22- or 23-course" omakase tasting menu at Sukiyabashi Jiro, the once* three-Michelin-starred sushi restaurant located in the cellar of an inconspicuous Tokyo office building. In 2007, Bourdain made a pilgrimage to

---

*In 2019, the Michelin Guide removed Sukiyabashi Jiro from its list, stripping it of its three stars, after the world-famous restaurant stopped accepting reservations from the general public in favor of catering to elite clientele.

this hallowed establishment to film the "Tokyo" episode of *No Reservations* (S4E16), where he met 82-year-old proprietor Jiro Ono, whom many believe to be the greatest sushi chef of all time, and savored the fruits of Ono's lifelong propensity for pescatarian perfectionism—an encounter that took place a full four years before the release of the 2011 documentary *Jiro Dreams of Sushi*.

What's that got to do with washing dishes? As Bourdain explains, this is a chef who, after some 75 years in the business, knows to serve every item at "exactly the right time and temperature and stage in its preparation." After indulging in a 15-course meal in the span of only 20 minutes—eating at Jiro's requires digging in right away, while the rice is perfectly warm—Bourdain asks the master if he "believes perfection is possible." To many, Jiro has already achieved this.

This is a man who instructed his staff to increase the time spent massaging the octopus from 30 to 45 minutes to achieve optimal texture and flavor. And his zealousness for technique extends beyond ingredients: The chef himself has admitted to observing which hand his customers use to pick up their sushi and adjusts his plating of each morsel according to their preference. It's nearly impossible to snag a reservation at his 10-seat restaurant, where celebrities and heads of state line up along the modest counter. Each diner can expect to pay at least $355 before tax, and it could be argued that Jiro could charge double or triple the amount. But he doesn't. It's a sobering thing to hear anyone, let alone someone in as challenging an industry as the restaurant business, announce, "We don't care about money."

Jiro's reply via translator to Bourdain's earlier question encapsulates the mindset of every devoted student of his or her craft: "There's no way of thinking that 'perfect' is something you ever actually attain." This sums up the spirit of the Japanese concept of shokunin, in which an apprentice takes pride in every task, especially menial ones. Take Jiro out of the kitchen and he is still a master because that's the last word he would ever use to describe himself.

When Bourdain, who hung up his apron after achieving overnight success with *Kitchen Confidential*, reminisces about his time as a dishwasher in a 2016 interview with NPR, you get the feeling he'd never refer to himself—or anyone—as a lowly dishwasher. Why? It's the first rung on the ladder of the business, a position in which, with a good work ethic, your only trajectory is up. Every unlearned lesson and unhoned skill stretches out before you as fresh as the day's produce. It's just you, some soapy water and the never-ending piles of crusted cookware and porcelain. Take a note from Bourdain: The true path to mastery lies in embracing the mundane and staying hungry for more.

Dining in China, 2005.

"Most chefs I know after work do not want to go out to dinner and be forced to think about what they're eating in a critical or analytical way. They want to experience food as they did as children, in an emotional way."

—NPR's *Fresh Air*, 2016

As Bourdain sees it, analyzing a meal doesn't inspire a deep-seated love of food. The dishes you turn to for comfort, the sort of fare your mother might have served after a rough day at school (in his case, this was cream of tomato soup)—these are what chefs gravitate toward: meals as a salve for the soul.

"Low
plastic stool,
cheap but
delicious noodles,
cold Hanoi beer."

—Anthony Bourdain, Twitter

THE BEST THINGS
ARE SIMPLE

BOURDAIN SET THE stage for his 2016 meeting with then-president Barack Obama over classic Vietnamese fare in the "Hanoi" episode of *Parts Unknown* (S8E1) with his trademark nonchalance. It's landmark television, seeing the leader of the free world slurping down street food on the other side of the globe. We're a long way from the elegance and posed photographs of a White House state dinner for a visiting dignitary. While settling into their bowls of bún cha, Obama remembers a favorite meal from his childhood: freshly caught fried fish served on a bed of rice, a dish so fundamentally uncomplicated that "nothing tasted so good." The meals— and by extension, moments—that matter most to you need not require snagging reservations a month in advance and donning chic smoking jackets or other pricey accoutrements. More doesn't always mean better.

Checking out the goods
in a kitchen in Sydney, 2005.

> "There is no lying in the kitchen.
> And no god there, either.
> He couldn't help you anyway."

—Medium Raw: A Bloody Valentine to the World of Food and the People Who Cook

---

In *Medium Raw*, the follow-up to his bestselling memoir *Kitchen Confidential*, Bourdain calls the kitchen "the last meritocracy"—a place where charm and guile fall away and where expertise alone determines whether or not a chef makes it through service. When it comes to gastronomy, whether you're hustling in a gleaming galley kitchen or hunched over a hot plate, everyone has a shot at making culinary magic happen. But the doing takes a dose of self-truth and requires the culling of self-delusion. It's always best to keep your knives, and skills, sharp.

"I never order fish on Monday unless I'm eating at Le Bernardin—a four-star restaurant where I know they are buying their fish directly from the source."

—Kitchen Confidential: Adventures in the Culinary Underbelly

COMPLIMENTS
ARE FREE

ANYONE WHO CAME to know and love Anthony Bourdain while he traveled the world making *No Reservations* and *Parts Unknown* might be shocked to discover he wasn't always best friends with Eric Ripert, the three-Michelin-starred executive chef and owner of the legendary restaurant Le Bernardin who dutifully accompanied Bourdain on many a trip. In fact, at the time he penned his ode to restaurant life, *Kitchen Confidential*, in 2000, Bourdain was little more than a raving fan. But that would soon change, all because he paid the man one hell of a compliment.

Unsure he'd be able to maintain employment in the industry once the dust had settled from unleashing his back-of-house tell-all on the unsuspecting public, Bourdain notes in the book's introduction that, come what may, his only goal is to present the life of a professional chef as he lived it, warts and all. The French chef, who in 1998 won his first James Beard Award, comes last in what can only be described as Bourdain's self-deprecating, absurd parade of best-case scenarios involving respected chefs fawning over him should the book prove successful: After invoking the likes of Emeril Lagasse, André Soltner and Bobby Flay, he adds that Ripert "won't be calling me for ideas on tomorrow's fish special." Later, as Bourdain explains how most restaurants receive their seafood on Fridays, he paints the picture of Ripert as the exception to a rule that people serve food long past its prime for the sake of turning a profit: "I never order fish on Monday unless I'm eating at Le Bernardin—a four-star restaurant where I know they are buying their fish directly from the source." It's an indictment of the industry at large, a stomach-churning shock to the system for most "civilians," as Bourdain described non-restaurant folk. But this banner praise of Ripert and his crew for flying in the face of a long-accepted standard in service of presenting the freshest ingredients possible did not go unnoticed.

This simple act—of giving kudos on a job well done—altered the course of Bourdain's life. Not long after the book hit shelves, Ripert got his hands on a copy. As he told *Hamptons Magazine* in 2012, "Seventy-five percent of the industry was saying, 'it's scandalous' and 'this guy is a disgrace.' Then part of the industry was saying, 'he's genius.' I called him and said, 'I read your book, and I would love to know you. Would you come for lunch?'" Their friendship lasted until Bourdain's death in 2018, which proved no small feat for a man who once told *The New Yorker*, "The kind of care and feeding required of friends, I'm frankly incapable of." Ripert, it seems, once again proved the exception to the rule. And five years after their initial meeting, Bourdain's idol-turned-friend set him up with a striking brunette, a host at one of his restaurants—Ottavia Busia, the woman who would later become Bourdain's wife and the mother of his only child, Ariane.

There are myriad reasons to get hung up on why you shouldn't give someone their flowers—perhaps you're concerned about how they'll receive your praise, or maybe you'd rather keep your head down and plug away at your to-do list. In an ideal world, though, paying someone a compliment should be as honest and automatic a reflex as sneezing (though decidedly more welcome in someone's face). A kind word can not only raise the spirits of the giver and receiver alike—it can also ripple through your life for years to come. Don't hold back.

> "You can't find the perfect meal.
> It finds you."
>
> —*No Reservations:*
> *Around the World on an Empty Stomach*

**Planning only gets you so far.
As Bourdain would have it, an excellent meal
begins not with the freshest ingredients
but rather an open mind. Allow yourself
the space to embrace the unexpected
and see where it takes you.**

BACK AGAIN !!
DOFINO LITE
HAVARTI
LOWER IN FAT THAN REGULAR

LEERDAMER
159

CHEESE
299

3.99
LB

Preparing to chow down at Mendel's Creamery in Toronto's Kensington Market, 2002.

"Always be on time."

—Men's Journal, 2014

SHOW UP ON TIME

ONSIDER THIS ONE of Anthony Bourdain's commandments. It's the measure by which he judged the people around him and the standard to which he held himself. Technically, he held himself to an even higher standard: As he explained to *Men's Journal*, by "on time," he means at least 15 minutes early. Given Bourdain's back-of-house roots, that's roughly enough time to prepare for the task at hand (the vegetables aren't going to peel themselves). He treated timeliness as a litmus test of "discipline, good work habits, and most importantly respect for other people." More than that, though, Bourdain considered someone's ability to arrive somewhere at a designated time a test of integrity. Arriving on time is an either/or binary: Either you value your commitments or you're "full of shit."

Touring the markets in China on April 26, 2005.

To Bourdain, travel was much more than a means of getting from point A to point B or, in extreme cases, hurtling headfirst into the unknown. In its most ideal state, the act of leaving what you know (or what you *think* you know) behind begins as a journey of the mind—a radical act of purging preconceptions. To embrace this method, you must be willing to accept the people and places you encounter exactly as you find them, which starts by freeing yourself of any pretense. It's the only way to avoid seeming pretentious.

"For the first and probably the last time, I sat next to the great man himself [Paul Bocuse], and Daniel [Boulud] and I were served a menu that chefs will look back on in a hundred years and smile at appreciatively, sentimentally, respectfully."

—*Parts Unknown*, "Lyon" (S3E3)

RESPECT THE CRAFT

BOURDAIN'S PUNK ETHOS wouldn't lead you to believe he knew his gastronomic history by heart, but nothing could be further from the truth. In the "Lyon" episode of *Parts Unknown* (S3E3), Bourdain visits one of the most important places in the world—at least as far as elevated Western cuisine is concerned—and pays homage to the greats who honed their craft in France's third-largest city. He unleashes his inner cooking geek with gusto while waxing poetic about the personalities that made French cooking the institution it is today.

"Over the past century," he explains in a voiceover, "the system, the tradition, whatever it is that took hold here churned out a tremendous number of the world's most important chefs." Their names roll off his tongue not unlike rock stars: Fernand Point, Alain Chapel, Jean and Pierre Troigros and Paul Bocuse. These men, along with the chefs they trained, are the originators of nouvelle cuisine, what even non-foodies might recognize is the now-industry standard of cooking, plating and serving elevated dishes rooted in simple ingredients and uncomplicated preparation. Bourdain's excitement is palpable as he sits down to dine with Chef Paul Bocuse, a living legend in the culinary world.

For longtime fans of Bourdain, the visual is somewhat surprising: his trademark uniform of blue jeans and a T-shirt? Gone. Instead, he's suited up, his face resplendent. But his choice of clothing and reserved reverence is only jarring if you don't know the context. In the same way that you wouldn't wear shorts to an audience with the pope, Bocuse—affectionately referred to as "the pope of gastronomy"—has more than earned Bourdain's deference and respect, not merely due to the mind-boggling quality of the meals he's served over the years but by his ability to mold and lead generations of chefs in pursuit of culinary excellence. This mission netted his L'Auberge du Pont de Collonges three Michelin stars for a staggering 55 years. Notably, he accomplished this by adhering to the kitchen hierarchy set out before him by Auguste Escoffier (the "king of chefs and chef of kings"), running a team with military-style precision, efficiency and cleanliness. As Bourdain explains in a voiceover, Bocuse's employees "live to avoid, under any circumstances, disappointing their comrades, the hierarchy or Monsieur Paul."

But even for all his numerous accolades, the then-88-year-old chef is quick to point out he, too, stands on the shoulders of giants. The walls of his restaurant are littered with the portraits of his predecessors. There's Fernand Point, widely regarded as one of the greatest chefs of all time and founder of Restaurant de la Pyramide, one of the most influential French restaurants to ever exist. And let's not forget Eugénie Brazier—aka "la Mère Brazier," the first chef to have a pair of three-Michelin-star restaurants. The tough-as-nails trailblazer trained a 20-year-old Bocuse and was, as the French chef recalls, "the first one up in the morning and the last one to go to bed."

Although Bocuse and Bourdain could not have lived more different lives outside of working hours, it's clear they are united by their love of delicious food and lasting memories of serving in "the system," as Bourdain calls the rigors of kitchen life. The lesson? Tipping your hat to those who paid their dues long before you is an act that transcends careers, language and culture. A large part of dedicating yourself to a craft is acknowledging, celebrating and, as necessary, humbling yourself before the innovators who put it on the map. If you can do that simply by wearing a suit and tie, all the better.

Enjoying himself over a lunch interview at Mai's Restaurant in Houston, Texas, 2002.

> "Life is complicated.
> It's filled with nuance.
> It's unsatisfying.... If I believe
> in anything, it is doubt."

—*Vogue*, October 21, 2016

Whether on or off camera,
Bourdain's mission was to understand why
people eat (or don't eat) the way they do.
Often, this meant confronting the multilayered
legacies of everything from colonialism to
systemic poverty to the military-industrial
complex. As he told *Vogue* in 2016,
"The root cause of all life's problems is looking
for a simple fucking answer." It's the synopsis
of a scene he revisited across Africa, Asia,
the Middle East and even at home in the U.S.
Take it from Bourdain: Question everything.

"There is nothing more political than food."

—*Variety*, August 5, 2014

FOOD AND HISTORY
ARE INSEPARABLE

I F A MEAL is more than the sum of its parts, then cuisine reflects more than an index of local staples and delicacies. As Bourdain was keen to point out, the act of eating always carries with it an element of sacrifice—the calf that was butchered, the farmer breaking his back in the field, the chef sweating in the boiling kitchen. But there are always other insidious forces at work when it comes to the meals that shape a community or region, and Bourdain highlighted these struggles, hardships and conflicts through his books and travel shows.

"I never make an overt decision to make a show political," Bourdain explained in a 2014 interview with *Variety*. "In fact, I try to avoid it. But there is nothing more political than food. If I'm there shoveling food in my face, it's worth mentioning who's not eating. If my host is missing three limbs, it's worth asking 'Hey, how'd ya lose them?'"

Nowhere is this more apparent than in the "Congo" episode of *Parts Unknown* (S1E8), in which Bourdain travels to a country that's seen the worst of what humanity has to offer across centuries, where detainment, extortion and threats of violence are a best-case—even daily—scenario next to murder and genocide. In an article on *CNN.com*, he explains how the Democratic Republic of the Congo "possesses the equivalent of trillions of dollars in resources: diamonds, gold, coltan (which the whole world requires for cell phones), minerals, timber, probably oil, uranium, and hydroelectric power. In short, it has everything that the First World needs and desires. This is its curse." This is a place where all that its people have endured is still playing out as the world gobbles up their natural resources, U.N. forces choke the streets and rebel groups plunge the encumbered populace into continual chaos.

In one sequence, Bourdain visits the Wagenya people, an indigenous fishing community living off the Congo River in Kisangani. He asks: Had they ever thought about how things might have been if they'd killed explorer Henry Morton Stanley, who essentially primed the country for the murderous King Leopold II of Belgium and the ensuing holocaust of some 10 million Congolese, rather than let him pass through? The reply is sobering in the extreme: "Someone else would have come." Notably, this conversation transpires before Bourdain partakes in the humblest of meals: limboke—tiger fish steamed in banana leaves—eaten with the hands. He explains in a voiceover that typically such a large fish would be sent to market in order to turn a profit. Instead, he's digging in as the guest of honor. It's a more-than-complicated moment: Bourdain, himself a Western outsider, is fully aware this act of hospitality comes to the detriment of the people he's visiting, a people whose way of life depends on a catch that in recent years has only dwindled. Yet he's in no place to reject such delicious generosity and risk offense. So he eats.

While "Congo" is hardly the only episode in which Bourdain explores how factors including but not limited to greed, famine, poverty, disease and imperialism can shape a nation and therefore its food, it's arguably the most stark. Never underestimate the story unfolding on your plate. Perhaps more importantly, never take it for granted.

> "A successful chef has to inspire
> great loyalty over time."

—Journeys in Artistry, June 27, 2006

In an industry still coming to grips with its legacy
of verbal and physical abuse, Bourdain's take on
what makes a great chef is a reminder
that a competent leader arrives early, stays late
and rallies the troops when morale dips.
No matter your field, your legacy is not defined
merely by your skill but by the lives you touch
along the way. All the more reason to make
sure the memories you leave behind
are positive ones.

In his natural habitat, aka the kitchen at Brasserie Les Halles.

"I love the sheer weirdness of the kitchen life: the dreamers, the crackpots, the refugees, and the sociopaths with whom I continue to work."

—"Don't Eat Before Reading This," *The New Yorker,* April 19, 1999

FIND YOUR PEOPLE

BEFORE HE ENROLLED in the Culinary Institute of America, Anthony Bourdain was a sullen teenager with a penchant for getting into trouble. As he once told Green Global Travel in an undated interview, "If I had a career trajectory, it was towards petty criminality." It wasn't until he took a summer job washing dishes at a seafood restaurant in Provincetown, Massachusetts, that he discovered a crew of misfits—dressed like pirates, no less—united under one unrelenting cause: making it through service. Years later, he dropped out of Vassar College to chase that community and camaraderie by making it his calling. No matter how you make your living, there's joy, inspiration and (in Bourdain's case) sometimes even money to be found in the company you keep. Choose well.

Preparing to savor a meal
in New York, 2007.

> "Don't drink at your hotel. Find out where the people who work at your hotel do their drinking."
>
> —*Bon Appétit*, May 9, 2016

As someone who prided himself on finding authentic eats no matter where his travels took him, Bourdain's advice on following the locals rings true for just about any activity. It can be tempting to stick with the familiar, comfortable or convenient, but this is not a winning strategy when it comes to finding the best experiences a city or town has to offer. Skip the sanitized, overpriced, tourist-approved digs and keep your eyes peeled. What you find might surprise you in the best possible way.

"Lesson number one as a traveler: Food given as a gesture of hospitality is always gratefully accepted. Always."

—No Reservations, "Namibia" (S3E4)

SHUT UP AND EAT

WHAT DOES IT look like to literally swallow your pride? For Anthony Bourdain, being a respectful guest meant humbling oneself at the altar of your host—the table—sacrificing any superficial personal preferences in the name of spreading goodwill. Plenty of moments filmed during the making of *No Reservations** and *Parts Unknown* bear witness to the strange, exotic and, occasionally, almost comically foul foods he subjected himself to in order to avoid insulting his hosts. Bourdain regarded this often painful shedding of the ego as a matter of respect for other cultures—a form of diplomacy. As an added bonus, practicing what he preached always made for compelling television.

Between the good, the bad and the ugly of what Bourdain

---

*Despite the braggadocio of his second show's title, Bourdain did, in fact, hold fast to a few reservations—notably, he refused to eat cats or dogs and was opposed to shark finning.

scarfed down on camera, it's this last category that stands out in terms of just how far he was willing to go to convey a noble message. When he sat down with Conan O'Brien to promote *A Cook's Tour: Global Adventures in Extreme Cuisine*s in 2002, Bourdain explained to the late-night host how one of the most vile things he'd ever eaten was undercooked iguana tamales. Never one to mince words, he likened it to "chewing on an action figure if you let it marinate in your childhood turtle tank." But this was early in his career, and there were many miles left to log before he'd stare down the two worst foods he'd ever consumed.

First, while filming the "Iceland: Hello Darkness My Old Friend" episode of *No Reservations* (S1E2), he managed to choke down a piece of hákarl. The Icelandic delicacy consists of Greenland shark that's been left to ferment for six months. It's also poisonous earlier in the preparation process. Chefs handling the meat wear gloves to avoid encountering the fish's high amounts of urea (it's a skin irritant), and the dish gives off the pungent aroma of ammonia ("a whiff of the crypt," as he later put it). It's edible only in the loosest definition of the word, yet Bourdain is quick to toss back a bite for the sake of his hosts.**

For Bourdain's worst meal ever, look to the "Namibia" episode of *No Reservations* (S3E4), where he accompanies

---

** He politely but firmly declined a second helping.

African bushmen on a hunt for a warthog. As their guest, Bourdain is given the most prized part of the animal—its unwashed rectum, cooked over hot coals until "al dente." But he wears no trace of horror or disgust as he watches them make quick work of the meat. Instead, he dutifully takes what is offered to him, grinning through every putrid bite.

Why did Bourdain put himself through the ringer time and again despite numerous voice-overs illustrating his displeasure and distress? He explains this put-yourself-last mentality, lovingly referred to as the "Grandma rule," in *Medium Raw*, in which he invokes the scene of sitting down to a poorly cooked Thanksgiving bird served by the family matriarch. "It may be overcooked and dry—and her stuffing salty and studded with rubbery pellets of giblet you find unpalatable in the extreme. You may not even like turkey at all. But it's Grandma's turkey. And you are in Grandma's house. So shut the fuck up and eat it."

Unless you plan on traveling to the far-flung corners of the globe in search of adventure, you will likely not be called upon to eat an unwashed warthog rectum in order to preserve the honor of your hosts. Which is to say, there are worse things than dry turkey. When you've got the good fortune of being a guest, sit back, relax and dig in with relish. If nothing else, do it for Grandma.

> "Who gets to tell the stories?
> This is a question asked often.
> The answer, in this case,
> for better or for worse, is I do."
>
> —*Parts Unknown*, "Kenya" (S12E1)

Bourdain was never shy to admit his race and background afforded him a relatively comfortable lifestyle compared to many of the people he encountered across his travels. The above quote is one of many examples in which he acknowledged his perspective and lived experience were entirely his own. Good intentions aside, it's not possible to walk a mile in someone else's shoes. Admitting that is the first step to understanding where someone else is coming from. Whether you're chatting with a noodle vendor in Vietnam or your neighbor across the street, knowing (and owning) your privilege—or lack thereof—is a key element of learning more about the world around you.

"Skills can be taught.
Character you either
have or don't have."

—*Kitchen Confidential*

DO IT RIGHT

NO DISH IS as brilliant a test of one's culinary prowess as the unassuming omelet. As Bourdain told *Playboy* in 2011, "The way you make an omelet reveals your character." Four ingredients—eggs, butter, salt and pepper—a nonstick pan and a preferred stirring utensil are all it takes to prove one's technical mastery at the stovetop. Er, almost: Knowing how to beat and stir the mixture, how to hold the pan as you coax the cooked curds onto a plate—these details transform a bowlful of yellow goop into fluffy nirvana. Being willing to do it with care and attention even if it's for the camper at table seven or a house guest who's overstaying their welcome—that's what separates the amateurs from the professionals. Doing something the right way for the right reasons is one of the hallmarks of good character. Any job that's worth doing is worth breaking a few literal or metaphorical eggs to do right.

At his restaurant,
Brasserie Les Halles,
in New York City, 2001.

—*Time*, October 31, 2007

No one is stopping you from eating
the same food you've always liked or strolling
down the same streets you've long haunted.
But why limit yourself? Curiosity—whether
about the tantalizing aromas wafting from the
food truck on your block or the story of how the
friendly faces running the plancha got their start
in the business—expands your lived experience
in more ways than you can readily measure.
It's not just about being a good neighbor:
It's about taking your place as
a citizen of the world.

"Perhaps the most important life lesson [my father] passed on was: Don't be a snob."

—*Bon Appétit*, 2012

DON'T BE A SNOB

OVER THE YEARS, especially after becoming a father in 2007, Anthony Bourdain frequently found moments to dispense wisdom passed down to him from his father. A self-described "man of simple needs," Pierre Bourdain was born to French parents, grew up in a francophone household and spent "many summers" in France, a country whose rich history of culinary excellence has by now been overstated and yet still falls short. He was also an executive for Columbia Records, and, for Bourdain, visiting his father's office in Manhattan meant availing himself of everything from street food like dirty-water hot dogs to highbrow fare. This latter category included visits to sushi restaurants which, to American palates in the 1970s, might as well have been as novel as walking on the moon. Perhaps most importantly, as Bourdain explains in a 2012 Father's Day essay for *Bon Appétit*, Pierre's lasting legacy to his firstborn can be summed up in four words of fatherly caution: "Don't be a snob."

You'd be forgiven for thinking Bourdain left this egalitarian approach to eating and living behind long ago—after all, he made a career out of visiting some of the finest restaurants in the world, including El Bulli, Sukiyabashi Jiro and The French Laundry. For someone so attuned to the trajectory of haute cuisine, who breathed the rarefied air of today's most renowned chefs and who made his home on New York's Upper East Side, it would be understandable to think Bourdain might have lived in something of a gastronomy bubble. But he also treasured his visit to Waffle House with Sean Brock in the "Charleston" episode of *Parts Unknown* (S6E9) and even came to the defense of a woman who'd given her own version of the Michelin star to one of the banes of Italian restauranteurs everywhere: Olive Garden.

At 85, Marilyn Hagerty had been a columnist at the *Grand Forks Herald* for more than a quarter of a century. Of her five* weekly columns, *The Eatbeat* saw her review area restaurants, and unlike far younger or more popular food critics across the internet, Marilyn never offered an unkind word or took a well-timed jab, even when a subpar meal might've warranted it. She didn't feel the need to antagonize anyone in her community by penning a negative review—

---

*As of 2024, the 98-year-old is still publishing a lifestyle column with the newspaper.

that wouldn't have been neighborly. So when Olive Garden, an Italian-adjacent casual chain restaurant, opened in Grand Forks, North Dakota, Marilyn took to her keyboard with the same clear-eyed enthusiasm as she would any other establishment. Among other notes, she praised its decor and the "warm and comforting" chicken Alfredo. Once it made its way to the internet, Marilyn's positive, unironic review did not sit well with food snobs and the Twitterati, who mocked her in droves. Marilyn went viral overnight.

But Bourdain saw something in the Midwestern reviewer: a journalist whose straightforward reporting came from a place of good intentions, someone dutifully fulfilling the obligations of her role who took pains not to say anything negative, ever. And someone who was definitively *not* a snob. Charmed and moved by her sincerity, Bourdain reached out with an offer to publish a collection of her writing. In 2013, his publishing imprint released *Grand Forks: A History of American Dining in 128 Reviews*. As he declared in the foreword, "This book kills snark dead." Snark and snobbery, though they might feed the ego, do not always feed the soul.

Bourdain's father got it right: Pleasure can be found in any dish, anywhere. "To experience joy, Bourdain writes in *Bon Appétit*, "one has to leave oneself open to it." Don't close yourself off from enjoying what lies ahead, no matter how humbly it presents itself.

> "Perhaps wisdom, at least for me,
> means realizing how small I am, and unwise,
> and how far I have yet to go."
>
> —*No Reservations*, "Peru" (S2E3)

You might be tempted to think the act of traveling will provide you with answers: about how others live, about your place in the world, about what sorts of living arrangements or conditions you're willing to endure.
And it might. But more importantly, engaging with different cultures and exotic locales will prompt you to ask questions you might not have otherwise wondered about.
You might even find, as Bourdain discovered, that there are few—if any—easy answers about how the world got to be the way it is.
Accepting that is a journey unto itself.

No Reservations, "Iceland: Hello Darkness My Old Friend" (S1E2).

"I believe that however you feel on whatever issue, we should always be able to sit down at a table together and have a few drinks—or a lot of drinks—and share a meal together."

—*Slate*, May 31, 2010

ESCAPE THE ECHO CHAMBER

MUCH HAS BEEN made about the outcome of the 2016 U.S. presidential election and how it transformed the way we approach those with whom we have political differences. Many have opted not to approach their fellow Americans at all. Anthony Bourdain was never shy about his loathing of Donald Trump and frequently took to Twitter to lambaste the businessman-turned-commander-in-chief. He did not, however, extend this animus to people who voted for him (as long as you weren't a politician, anyway). Nowhere is this more readily or freakishly apparent than in 2008's "U.S. Southwest" episode of *No Reservations* (S4E15), which highlights Bourdain's budding friendship with his political opposite: hard rock guitarist Ted Nugent. Granted, in the aftermath of Trump's first term, with hate speech on the rise and social media echo chambers amplifying rage to a fever pitch, 2008 feels like an incredibly naïve time. But it shows how far Bourdain was willing to go—literally and metaphorically—to break bread with people with whom he didn't see eye-to-eye.

"Outspoken" is too mild a word to describe the man behind the hit 1977 single "Cat Scratch Fever." Uncle Ted, as the rock star is known to fans, is the fired-up exclamation point at the end of Bourdain's road trip from L.A. to the Lone Star State. Like Bourdain, the Nuge can be described as a provocateur, ready to unload his (wildly conservative) opinion at any given moment. And fire away he does, so much so that in 2012, the Secret Service investigated Nugent in response to his inflammatory comments about then-president Barack Obama. But even though the gun-toting guitar legend and outspoken hunting advocate sits about as far right as Bourdain does left (if not more so), the two find common ground while bowhunting, firing automatic weapons and having a few beers by the grill at Nugent's ranch near Waco, Texas.

Swept up in Nugent's "borderline sociopathic charm," Bourdain describes the musician as "scary smart, funny as hell, intermittently kind and philanthropic" as the two tour Nugent's sprawling wildlife preserve. Politically opposed ideologies dissolve into the background as Bourdain and Nugent observe a herd of oryx (a type of antelope) charging through the bush. Nugent comes off as passionate about the planet's renewable resources, even if his voting record might say otherwise. He also takes a vested personal interest in hosting wounded Iraq War veterans at his estate, inviting them on hunts as a sort of primal scream-based therapy. By the time Bourdain picks Nugent's brain over brisket at the local barbecue joint, the two have managed to agree on a number of points, including treating hunted animals with respect and a shared concern over a rise in childhood obesity.

Two years after the episode aired, Bourdain reflected on their meeting in a 2010 interview with *Slate*: "I disagree with everything Ted Nugent says, but I like the guy a lot." The feeling was mutual. After news broke that Bourdain had taken his own life, Nugent acknowledged his passing on Twitter, writing, "Adios & Godspeed my kill it & grill it bloodbrother."

Bourdain's travels through what his self-described "lefty comrades" might call flyover country reveal a singular truth: No matter your beliefs, it's nearly impossible to find someone with whom you have nothing in common. Sharing a meal with someone is an endorsement of that individual's humanity. There's nothing to gain from staying holed up in your own echo chamber. A slab of brisket isn't going to bring our nation together. But finding common ground over good food can at least bridge the gap.

Anthony Bourdain
in an undated photo.

> **"Luck is not a business model."**
>
> *—Medium Raw*

Bourdain was always quick to point out how fortunate he was—to beat his drug addiction and to become a published author and making a career out of eating all over the world. But the truth is that discipline and a solid work ethic accounted for 99 percent of his career and personal success. It was also not lost on him that he didn't begin to live what anyone would call a comfortable life until the age of 43, having squandered much of his youth in pursuit of the next fix. He's fortunate to have avoided missing out on even more, but luck wasn't the primary ingredient in his success. There's little use in hoping your dreams will come to fruition if you aren't willing to put in the mileage. Devote your resources and focus accordingly.

"Schedule your hangover."

—Men's Journal, 2014

DISCIPLINE GETS IT DONE

AS A RECOVERING addict, Bourdain drew a clear line between what he was and was not willing to do to unwind. While the chef kicked heroin cold turkey, he notably did not give up drinking. But don't think that alcohol dominated his downtime. As Bourdain explained to *Men's Journal* in 2014, despite the abundance of bacchanalia footage in *Parts Unknown*, he took a teetotaler approach while at home with family: "I don't ever drink in my house." Bourdain knew he'd accomplished too much—as a boss, husband and father—to risk letting himself screw it up. Whatever job you need to do, whether that's putting dinner on the table literally or metaphorically, set your boundaries and stick to them.

Savoring the spoils from Chef Ludo Lefebvre's LudoTruck in Los Angeles while exploring the city for an episode of *The Layover*.

> "Why should you be excited about food trucks? Because they allow creative chefs, without a lot of money, to start creating and selling their stuff."
>
> —*Parts Unknown*, "Los Angeles" (S1E2)

When it comes to cheap, tasty, accessible eats, look no further than the humble food truck. Sure, these kitchens on wheels aren't anchored in a brick-and-mortar setup, but as Bourdain explains, that's the point. Free from overhead costs, food trucks are the fastest way (literally) for up-and-coming chefs to get their menus to the masses, interfacing with customers anywhere they can park. This isn't just a call to embrace a city's fleet of moveable feasts—it's a reminder that delicious dishes and prompt service need not be confined to white tablecloths. Save your judgment for the food.

"Of all the places,
of all the countries,
all the years of traveling,
it's here, in Iran, that I am
greeted most warmly
by total strangers."

—*Parts Unknown*, "Iran" (S4E6)

SPEAK UP

P ART OF ANTHONY Bourdain's enduring appeal lies in his willingness to document people and places as he found them. It's how he built a sizable fan base all over the world. Of all the locations he had the opportunity to visit, none made a more lasting positive impression than Iran. But this bright spot in his television career was soon marred by fear—that two of his guides would be silenced by an authoritarian government, all because he showcased their honest insights about their beloved country.

"Words matter," Bourdain wrote on the *Parts Unknown* website. "Especially in Iran, where what is permissible—to say, to do, to be seen to say or do—is an ever-changing thing." Just 13 minutes into "Iran," Bourdain explains in a voiceover that two of his hosts whom he met for lunch in Tehran had been imprisoned. The American-born *Washington Post* correspondent Jason Rezaian and his

Iranian wife, journalist Yeganeh Rezaian, were arrested and detained weeks after a fateful interview discussing life in Iran over grilled meat. As with most arrests made by the Islamic Republic, the charges were trumped up—in this case, espionage on behalf of the United States. The regime let Yeganeh go after 10 weeks. Her husband was not so fortunate. Amidst scenes of young Iranians showing off souped-up vintage American cars and eating pizza with ketchup, "Iran" ends on the ominous note that Rezaian's future remains unclear.

Bear in mind this is the same extremist regime that sent assassins abroad to kill author Salman Rushdie's translators and publishers after his work, *The Satanic Verses*, was deemed blasphemous of Islam.* According to Reporters Without Borders, Iran is the fourth most inhospitable country in the world to journalists. Bourdain knew he'd have to act fast to save his interviewee from an unthinkable fate.

He published an op-ed in *The Washington Post* insisting on the couple's innocence and expressing concern for Rezaian's safety. He writes, "two more kind, positive and open-minded ambassadors of understanding could hardly be imagined.... I am, of course, deeply worried for the both of them. They seem to have dropped off the face of the

---

*Since 2012, the bounty for killing Rushdie has been set to $3.3 million dollars.

Earth. No communication. No reasons given. Just gone." He then appeared on *Anderson Cooper 360* with Rezaian's brother, Ali, to plead for his release, and took to Facebook to post about the Rezaians' perilous predicament.

Strangely enough, the very thing that put a target on the couple hastened their eventual reunion. As CNN correspondent Brian Stelter put it, the *Parts Unknown* footage "actually helped television reporters cover the news of his detainment." After a grueling 544 days, diplomacy won out via the State Department: Rezaian was freed as part of a prisoner exchange.

Shortly after Bourdain's death, Rezaian explained to CNN that Bourdain's support didn't end the moment Rezaian left prison: He "[counseled] us privately in our interactions with him, professionally but also how to get through what was really a tough reintegration." In 2019, Rezaian released his memoir, *Prisoner*, with the chef's publishing imprint, a posthumous endorsement of the Iran Rezaian knew and loved. That Rezaian survived (and doesn't regret filming the show) is as much a testament to his convictions as it is the tenacity of the people who sought to free him. Iran defied Bourdain's expectations, and he went out of his way to ensure fellow truth-tellers would survive imprisonment. The lesson: When you have a public platform, use it for good, with ethics and solidarity in mind.

No Reservations,
"Berlin" (S3E12).

"If you're twenty-two, physically fit, hungry to learn and be better, I urge you to travel—as far and as widely as possible. Sleep on floors if you have to. Find out how other people live and eat and cook. Learn from them—wherever you go."

—*Medium Raw*

Don't think Bourdain's advice only applies to twentysomethings. If you do find yourself in that sweet spot of early adulthood, before the ennui of middle age sets in, consider yourself lucky: You've got a head start on widening your horizons before familial or business obligations anchor you elsewhere. If not, Bourdain's words are sure to shake you out of your to-do list stupor. There's no expiration date on learning "how other people live and eat and cook," just your willingness to wonder what makes other people tick. Harness the power of curiosity and let it fuel your voyages into the unfamiliar.

"[Butter] is usually the first thing and the last thing in just about every pan. That's why restaurant food tastes better than home food a lot of the time."

—*The Oprah Winfrey Show*, 2001

THE SECRET INGREDIENT IS BUTTER

THERE'S A REASON amateur cooks get frustrated trying to recreate their favorite restaurant meals in the comfort of home. As Bourdain explained to Oprah Winfrey on her eponymous talk show in 2001, it's because chefs use sinful, artery-clogging amounts of butter in nearly every dish. According to Bourdain, by the time you've left after dining at a "classic French restaurant," you've probably ingested more than a stick of butter. But if this knowledge comes as a calorie-laden shock to you, let it serve as a lesson. Occam's razor holds true in the kitchen: What tastes too good to be true is probably swimming in liquid gold. You don't know what you don't know. Don't beat yourself up. Just add a bit of butter.

Posing for photographer
Jacky Chapman.

"[W]atch movies, read everything you can. Be inspired by what others have done and learn from their mistakes. Stealing is fine as long as you can reasonably suggest it was just 'borrowing' in court."

—*In the Weeds* by Tom Vitale

In 2021, Bourdain's longtime director and producer, Tom Vitale, published *In the Weeds*, a memoir of his time working under his globe-trotting boss. He cites Bourdain's directive for living well in the quote above, showing how the chef was prone to devour much more than food. A rich life isn't defined by exotic vistas and world-class cuisine (well, not exclusively, anyway). It begins with giving your mind something substantial to chew on.

"I blame my first oyster for everything I did after: my decision to become a chef, my thrill-seeking, all my hideous screwups in pursuit of pleasure. I blame it all on that oyster. In a nice way, of course."

—*A Cook's Tour: Global Adventures in Extreme Cuisines*

GOOD FOOD IS ABOUT RISK

YOU'VE GOT TO wonder about the first human who decided to eat an oyster. There's little appeal in terms of the bivalve mollusk's rock-like outward appearance. Dark, ridged shells don't look particularly appetizing. Inside's somehow worse. Pry the thing open and come face to face with the gray glob of mucilaginous flesh staring back at you. Tip it down the hatch, raw, unseasoned, without a second thought. This is precisely what Bourdain did in his youth while spending a summer in France, and slurping down this risky food set him on a path he never dreamed of.

He recounts the moment vividly in *Kitchen Confidential*, setting a scene wherein he, his parents and little brother are invited out on an oyster boat off the coast of southwest France by their neighbor, an oyster fisherman he calls Monsieur Saint-Jour. When Bourdain complains of hunger (complaining being a common theme of his adolescence), Saint-Jour asks if anyone would care to try an oyster. Three of the four passengers shift uncomfortably—mother and father, although obsessed with the cutting-edge haute cuisine served at La Pyramide to the point that they'd leave their sons in the car to enjoy their meal, are inconspicuously silent. Apparently, they draw the line at oysters. Younger brother Christopher recoils in horror. But Bourdain seizes this moment to defy and gross out his folks—he volunteers to eat one, much to Saint-Jour's delight. "I'd not only survived," he writes, "I'd enjoyed." Somewhere, between the pulpy, briny flesh, the taste of seawater, the joy of shocking his loved ones, rising to a challenge and dutifully accepting Saint-Jour's generosity, Bourdain came into his own.

What the chef-in-the-making learned at a tender age is that living well demands risk. There's a chance any new food you try will make you sick. Oysters, it should be noted, are still alive up to five minutes after being shucked. It's this freshness that can prevent a host of illnesses from ruining your night out. As with other shellfish, oysters filter water, so it follows that bacteria from the area where the creatures were harvested, or from improper handling, can wreak quite a bit of havoc: namely, vibriosis, norovirus infection and hepatitis A. Cooking oysters kills off this bacteria, sure—if you need to be absolutely certain.* But that changes the texture. It also robs you of the opportunity to pluck them from the seabed and scarf them down as Bourdain did off the coast of southwest France. Which would've made for a pretty forgettable fishing trip, bracing views of the Atlantic notwithstanding.

It's a lesson Bourdain lived and preached across every sphere of his life, especially when traveling: There's a far better story to be told when you take a chance and let the chips fall where they may. As he told *Newsweek* in 2016, worst comes to worst, "You're looking at a long course of antibiotics…. [Foodborne illness] is a really small price to pay for all the really awesome food that I've had and the kind of relationships I've been able to have with people."

Yes, there will be gastrointestinal distress. The meat, at some point, will be undercooked, the vegetables unwashed. The plane could crash during take-off, the car in the oncoming lane could jump the median and come barreling at you. While walking in a city, your chance of craning your neck skyward only to spot a piano dangling above you by a frayed rope is never zero. But all catastrophizing does is rob you of the chance to see everything that could go gloriously, deliciously well.

Life's too short to live in fear. Shuck it.

---

*According to the Virginia Department of Health, "millions" of Americans enjoy oysters and clams each year—just steer clear of eating them raw if you've got a weakened immune system.

"People are put on Earth
for various purposes;
I was put on Earth
to do this.
Eat noodles right here."

—*Parts Unknown*, "Vietnam" (S4E4)

FIND YOUR PURPOSE

BOURDAIN'S ONLY BEING a smidge hyperbolic in the "Vietnam" episode of *Parts Unknown* when he says his raison d'être is slurping down strings of starch by the bowlful. The former chef carved out a life for himself informed by devouring delicious food, encountering generous people and visiting so many countries that he burned through a whopping 12 passports, "livin' the dream" in the most unironic fashion. It's a lesson worth picking up no matter your milieu. Knowing yourself well enough to lean on your strengths, then chasing the things that bring you joy are the key ingredients for maximizing your potential. Spurn the sin of mediocrity. Time is too limited to do anything less.

Footage from *Roadrunner: A Film About Anthony Bourdain* (2021).

> "Under 'Reasons for Leaving Last Job,' never give the real reason, unless it's money or ambition."
>
> —*Kitchen Confidential*

Bourdain packs his magnum opus full of hard-earned wisdom, including a heaping helping of sound career advice. The above one-liner applies to just about any field: When it comes to nailing your job application and interview game, oversharing does far more to hurt your chances than help them. But this bon mot isn't about positivity—it's about portraying your career trajectory and personality in the best light possible. That starts with knowing what to keep to yourself.

"I'm no marine biologist, but I know dead octopus when I see one.... Strangely, everyone else pretends to believe the hideous sham unfolding before our eyes, doing their best to ignore the blindingly obvious."

—*Parts Unknown*, "Sicily" (S2E5)

EMBRACE
AUTHENTICITY

"**S**ICILY" ISN'T SO much an episode of *Parts Unknown* as it is one man's account of what it takes to push through a nervous breakdown. The Italian island is the one location that bested Anthony Bourdain's storytelling abilities not once but twice during his career. Between the rich history, stunning views, plentiful *Godfather* references (this is, after all, where Michael Corleone married Apollonia Vitelli) and delicious cuisine, creating episodes here should be a breeze. Except it's not. Bourdain's earnest desire to show people as they are, his struggle to swim upstream against a current of absurdity and lies, isn't just an existential crisis— it's what set him apart as an artist in search of the real.

In a fishing scene, our hero first notices something's amiss when his host, a local fisherman and chef named Turi, takes him to look for octopus and cuttlefish off a busy beach. A bay full of party boats and lively swimmers doesn't seem conducive to fishing, but surely Turi knows what he's doing, right? Bourdain continues the voiceover:

"So I get in the water and I'm paddling around—and splash. Suddenly there's a dead sea creature sinking slowly to the seabed in front of me.... Splash. There's another one, another rigor mortis, half-frozen freakin' octopus. But it goes on, one dead cuttlefish, deceased octopus, frozen sea urchin after another, splash, splash, splash."

It's not enough that Bourdain's host is clumsily staging a fishing trip by stocking the waters with store-bought seafood—Turi then hooks an octopus and shows it off to the camera, smiling as though he'd just speared it himself while it was alive, not frozen. After a few minutes, Turi dumps in a whole bag of dead sea creatures. "For some reason, I feel something snap," Bourdain says, "and I slide quickly into a spiral of near hysterical depression." It's also his birthday. Cue the meltdown.

"Things fall apart," W.B. Yeats declares in his 1919 poem "The Second Coming." Written in the aftermath of the First World War, the chaos translates well to Bourdain's inward battle to maintain civility and decorum in the face of blatant deception. "Mere anarchy is loosed upon the world.... The ceremony of innocence is drowned" as Bourdain, bobbing in the waves, grapples with what to make of his predicament. What is there left to say about the integrity of Turi, himself a chef, as he repeatedly slaps an octopus against rocks on the beach to tenderize its chilled flesh? How can Bourdain trust anything this man says or does? The fishing trip casts a pall over the rest of his stay that not even a reported 18 negronis can wash away. As he later told *Forbes* in 2016, "I don't go out there looking to make a funny show mocking this well-meaning but thoroughly corrupt fisherman who was just trying to make things entertaining." If "Hell is other people," as Jean-Paul Sartre put it, then this episode shows Bourdain swan-diving into the flames. Liquor aside, "Sicily" is an exercise in self-control. It's a hilarious (if tragicomic) example of what Bourdain struggled with in order to make a television show that avoids artifice and fakery.

In this age of highly manipulated and curated media, when influencers tell you what to buy, where to go and what to eat, what's the point of chasing what's real? Whatever is inconvenient, painful, laborious or just plain tedious— these are the things that add friction and flavor to our days, shaping our interactions with others and our outlook on the world. Your search for meaning may not take the shape you hoped for. But it can still make for quite the story later.

Parts Unknown,
"Montana" (S7E4).

> "I once wrote, 'Your body isn't a temple,
> it's an amusement park. Enjoy the ride.'
> But that was before I had a daughter
> and a respectable job at CNN."
>
> —*Parts Unknown*, "Thailand" (S3E7)

Priorities change. And with them, so do your responsibilities. What you once might've shaken off with a couple of hours' sleep, a venti coffee and a double dose of aspirin might derail your weekend once you have a precocious, shrieking toddler to answer to. Bourdain isn't saying you've got to give up playing hard—only that you owe it to the people who depend on you to know your limits. Even amusement parks require maintenance.

"It's a successful series for me if someone who liked the show last week tunes in this week, and is uncertain whether they're on the right channel."

—*Variety*, August 5, 2014

GET WEIRD

I T'S AUGUST 16, 2010. President Barack Obama isn't quite halfway through his first term in office. Spain is still riding the vuvuzela-punctuated high of winning the FIFA World Cup in South Africa. Millions of gallons of oil are leaking from an oil rig in the Gulf of Mexico, coating beaches from Florida to Texas in tar— an ecological disaster of never-before-seen proportions. Anyone tuning into the Travel Channel that evening for a bit of exotic, colorful escapism involving food instead finds something filmed entirely in black and white. This, the "Rome" episode of *No Reservations* (S6E20), was my first clue that Anthony Bourdain had much more in mind than breezy entertainment.

Well, OK, maybe not the first clue—there was, after all, the "Beirut" episode (S2E14) four years prior, a foray into journalism-laced television in which his film crew witnessed the outbreak of the Lebanon War. But that was about making the most out of a tense, frightening moment. Instead, this Federico Fellini homage was, one might say, years in the making for the dedicated cinephile. As he told *IndieWire* days before he took his own life in 2018, "I'd probably seen the entire Janus Films collection by the time I was 12. My parents were the sort of people who went to theaters to see Bergman and Antonioni. Filmmakers were respected in my house from the beginning."

With its stark visual aesthetic, "Rome" is a love letter to Fellini's 1960 classic *La Dolce Vita* starring Marcello Mastroianni. In one sequence, Bourdain, wearing sunglasses and a skinny tie like the cool, detached playboy protagonist, retraces the steps of the modernist masterpiece, even sidling up to the Trevi Fountain to contemplate life. The first dish he tears into plays into this artistic palette: cacio e pepe, that sublime Roman specialty of spaghetti, pecorino and freshly ground pepper. Who'd ever thought to make a food show a study in chiaroscuro? But Bourdain goes further. Where other travel programs feel like bloated advertisements dripping with commercialism (looking at you, Samantha Brown), this episode does the opposite: Bourdain withholds the names of every restaurant he visits, lest he "kill" what he loves with flocks of hungry fans. It's a hipster's dream and nightmare wrapped into one. He also indulges his love of phony driving scenes in old movies: Bourdain rents a 1966 Alfa Romeo and films in front of a green screen, jerking the wheel constantly while Eternal City B-roll traffic footage plays behind him smoother than gelato. Suffice it to say, you're just not going to get this kind of highbrow, lowbrow (even a bit of slapstick) mix anywhere else.

With his career-defining move to CNN in 2013, Bourdain gained a substantial budget to do even more with his art, this time in the form of *Parts Unknown*. Over the years, he racked up quite the roster of star collaborators, including Darren Aronofsky, Francis Ford Coppola, Abel Ferrara and Vilmos Zsigmond. "I like things to be strange and beautiful and, if and when possible, not done before," he told *GQ* in 2017. "I'd rather fail gloriously and foolishly than turn in efficient and adequate work again and again." It's no wonder, then, that this ambitious approach netted him a cool seven Emmys in 12 seasons of *Parts Unknown*—he made episodes with events presented in reverse ("Korea," S5E1), dream sequences ("Thailand," S3E7) and much, much more.

Whatever you put your mind to, whether for work or, well, pasta, you do yourself a disservice by phoning it in. Get weird and see where it takes you.

Parts Unknown,
"Myanmar" (S1E1).

"There's a guy inside me who wants to lay in bed, and smoke weed all day, and watch cartoons, and old movies.... My whole life is a series of stratagems to avoid, and outwit, that guy."

—*Men's Journal*, 2014

Each of us has a siren song—a dark desire that calls out in moments of stress or boredom, usually as a means of procrastination. Whether you share Bourdain's desire to curl up indoors and lose yourself in the void of television or you're more of the outdoorsy, extroverted persuasion, living a life you're proud of means staying a few steps ahead of the things that, when left to your own devices, would drag you into a comfortable lull. Rest when you need to, but don't linger so long that you lose sight of what sparks your curiosity.

"I became a father at fifty years of age....
At no point previously had I been old enough, settled enough, or mature enough for this, the biggest and most important of jobs: the love and care of another human being."

—*Appetites: A Cookbook*

MAKE TIME
FOR FAMILY

FATHERHOOD WAS SOMEWHAT of a curveball for
Bourdain. For most of his life, it simply hadn't been
a priority, and it's easy to see why. Between working
long shifts in kitchens and scrambling to score on the Lower
East Side, the chef was hardly in a place to be paternal. In
the roughly 20 years Bourdain spent with his high school
sweetheart and first wife Nancy Putkoski, ambition had
not been part of the plan, let alone children. Filming his
first show, *A Cook's Tour*, spelled the end of the marriage—
Nancy didn't care for the limelight nor the time away from
home. The two divorced in 2005.

Fast forward to July 2006. At 50, the chef had been
working on a second travel program, *No Reservations*,
and had begun dating an associate of Eric Ripert's, Ottavia
Busia. If filming the outbreak of war in Beirut upended
Bourdain's view of what he could accomplish with his

career, fathering a child would similarly reconfigure how he viewed himself as a person.

Conceived shortly after Bourdain returned to New York from his harrowing experience in Lebanon, Ariane Busia-Bourdain was born on April 9, 2007. In numerous interviews, he describes seeing her "corkscrew out of the womb" as the moment that prompted him to "make adjustments" in his life. Where some people might find themselves stuck in their ways by the tail end of their midlife years, Bourdain threw himself into his new role with gusto. Early-morning diaper changes? Bring it on. Brunch, once the bane of his existence, a humiliating fallback job he could always count on, was now a chance to teach Ariane the tricks of the trade. As a parent, flipping pancakes meant debuting "Dada's Bespoke Pancake Bar" while hosting sleepovers, as he shared on Twitter.

And where most parents might grow tired of the monotony, for Bourdain, coming home proved to be a relief. As someone who spent a grueling 250 days on the road on average, he made sure to always devote roughly five a month to be with his family. It also meant he relished any excuse to practice the mundane tasks many of us take for granted. Conscientious of his fame, he was careful to preserve his daughter's privacy, always obscuring her face in photographs. Careful eyes can spot Ariane in his later work, notably *Appetites: A Cookbook*, and she even provides a voiceover in the "Iran" episode of *Parts Unknown*, narrating a fairy-tale version of the country's history with regard to U.S. interventionism.

"There's a picture of me and my daughter, aged four, in the Cayman Islands," Bourdain writes of his progeny in a 2013 essay for *The Guardian*. "She's sitting on my lap, eyes closed. I'm holding her tight, my face sunburned and blissed-out with the joys of fatherhood. Ariane has me wrapped around her finger. All I can realistically hope for is that she feels loved." He was 57 when he wrote those words, the same age his father was when he died in 1987. Pierre Bourdain didn't live long enough to see his son turn his life around. The chef, it seems, was keen to make the most of the time he could carve out with his only child.

By no means does family have to include the people by whom you were raised. For most of his life, Bourdain's family, to a large extent, comprised the kitchen staff with whom he worked. You don't have to be a parent to know creating memories with loved ones is one of the best parts of life.

Food tour through China,
April 26, 2005.

> "No one understands and appreciates the American Dream of hard work leading to material rewards better than a non-American."
>
> —*Kitchen Confidential*

From his first summer gig washing dishes in Provincetown, Bourdain rolled up his sleeves alongside people from all walks of life, many of whom were not born in the States. "Should you become a leader," he advises readers in *Kitchen Confidential*, "Spanish is absolutely essential." Whether on- or off-camera, Bourdain championed the tenacity of his fellow kitchen staff who toiled behind hot stoves to eke out a better life for themselves than they would've had back home.

For those who share Bourdain's middle-class background, it's a reminder that immigrants have always made America great.

"Regret is something you've got to just live with, you can't drink it away. You can't run away from it. You can't trick yourself out of it. You've just got to own it."

—Men's Journal, 2014

OWN YOUR MISTAKES

ADDICTION DOES NOT occur inside a vacuum. When the search for the next high has you sinking to new lows, more often than not, other people get caught in the crosshairs. Whenever he spoke about his years shooting heroin, Anthony Bourdain didn't mince words: He was no stranger to hurting others. Turning his life around didn't automatically rectify the lies and broken relationships left in his fiery wake, either. "[T]hat's just something I'm going to have to live with," he told *Men's Journal* in 2014. Don't go looking to blame others for the fallout from the poor choices you made. "[E]at that guilt," Bourdain cautions, and accept whatever comes next.

"I'm stuck in a vast old Victorian hotel with endless rooms and hallways trying to check out, but I can't. I spend a lot of time in hotels, but this one is menacing because I just can't leave it. And then there's another part to this dream, always, where I'm trying to go home but I can't quite remember where that is."

—*Parts Unknown*, "Buenos Aires" (S8E8)

EVERYONE HAS A STRUGGLE

HOW DOES IT feel to have the greatest job in the world? For many people, it looked a lot like what Anthony Bourdain did for a living: flying all over the world to places most of us only dream of visiting, savoring incredible food made by fascinating people we'll almost certainly never meet. Much of the time, Bourdain himself was inclined to agree. It sure beat serving brunch. That doesn't mean it was all cocktails and rainbows. The occasional trip is a luxury, a welcome escape from the ordinary. Spending 250 days a year away from home, on the other hand, is sure to take a toll on even the most enthusiastic of travelers.

For Bourdain, the constant movement, brutal workload and stress of coordinating dangerous shoots intensified feelings of isolation. Even eating a bad burger at an airport could send him into a tailspin of depression, something he brings up in the "Buenos Aires" episode of *Parts Unknown*. Bourdain books a session with a psychologist (which are popular in Argentina) and reveals some disturbing dreams have been plaguing him. Longtime fans are well aware of his various neuroses and past battle with addiction, which he makes no effort to hide. But "Buenos Aires" shows the chef baring his innermost thoughts on camera to a mental health professional. Prior to this moment, he's framed any morbid talk as a joke.

What could possibly feel like home when you're away most of the year? It's why a bad experience at Johnny Rockets proves nothing less than soul-crushing to Bourdain, something he cites as the reason for booking the therapy session to begin with. A meal—in this case, a burger—made without care, reheated in the most pathetic way, mass-produced and served to him by people who'd rather be anywhere else—nothing could be more antithetical to everything he stood for and believed in. Why bother with anything?

Let's make one thing abundantly clear: Bourdain was the first to admit how fortunate he was to have such a cushy, privileged job. It afforded him the chance to rub elbows with industry giants, such as Eric Ripert, who became his best friend, flex his considerable writing talents—whether in the script or on his blog—and crack clever jokes on television. None of that negates the fact that when the cameras were off he still had demons to face.

In truth, there are myriad takeaways from this episode. Some were apparent when it aired in 2016, others more so when watching it after his death in 2018. One session of therapy can't "fix" or heal anyone. That's not how it works. Self-reflection takes real effort. It requires vulnerability and transparency, both of which can be painful, but its insights can prove invaluable if you're willing to put in the time. Though Bourdain is mostly remembered for exposing viewers to people, places and meals they'd never experienced, this episode is a testament to his desire to also look inward.

Don't assume that because someone works hard and looks put together, they've got it all figured out or that nothing keeps them up at night. Not everyone struggles in the same way, and not every battle is readily visible.

"Everyone should
see how complicated,
how deeply troubled,
and yet, at the same time,
beautiful and awesome
the world can be."

—*Parts Unknown*, "Beirut" (S5E8)

BAD THINGS HAPPEN TO GOOD PEOPLE

BENEATH ANTHONY BOURDAIN'S hardened exterior beat the heart of an idealist. Sure, he'd been through the wringer as an addict and a line cook, no stranger to the extremes people use to fill the void. But this first half of his life didn't deaden his sense of what makes life worth living—if anything, it heightened it. Just because trouble and misfortune are certain to befall everyone at some point doesn't negate the presence of all that's nourishing, life-affirming or lovely. "Bad things happen to good people all the time," he wrote on CNN.com in an essay introducing *Parts Unknown*. "When they do, hopefully, you'll have a better idea who, and what, on a human scale, is involved."

"We are clearly at a long overdue moment in history where everyone, good hearted or not, will HAVE to look at themselves, the part they played in the past, the things they've seen, ignored, accepted as normal, or simply missed—and consider what side of history they want to be on in the future."

—*Medium*, December 12, 2017

Whenever Bourdain discusses "the system," the backbreaking kitchen hierarchy that often thrives on verbal and physical abuse, you get the impression he's witnessed countless great and terrible things in pursuit of culinary excellence. And then, as any student of history knows, there's the twinge that comes with knowing Bourdain himself was a product of said boys' club. At least he didn't let it hold him back from attempting to right the ship later in life. Doing the right thing isn't just about calling others out but also holding yourself to account.

"There are times that I have looked at the camera and said, look, I'm just not going to tell you where this place is. It's too good, and I don't want to change it. It should stay like this forever."

—NPR's *Fresh Air*, 2016

DON'T BROADCAST EVERYTHING

ONE OF THE most enduring images fans hold of Anthony Bourdain is the lanky, foul-mouthed television host gazing out against a foreign backdrop wearing Persol sunglasses. It's the sort of scene usually accompanied by a voiceover, one that often begins with a question or a single word meant to encapsulate his impressions of a place, whether dazzling or disorienting. In these shots, excellent cinematography notwithstanding, Bourdain sees without being seen (er, without meeting the viewer's gaze), his brooding mind holed up behind acetate frames as a camera crew follows him to yet another far-flung locale. As his viewership grew, especially after making the move to CNN in 2013, Bourdain knew he couldn't allow packs of raving (if preternaturally observant) fans to disrupt the delicate ecosystems of his favorite digs. So the travel host did something virtually unheard of: He began withholding the names of restaurants and bars he visited on his show.

For a mom-and-pop business to receive the coveted Bourdain seal of approval was a double-edged sword. On the one hand, his compliments on a particular dish, chef, ambience or all of the above—whether captured on camera or penned online—would all but guarantee a steady stream of foot traffic, not just saving a family's livelihood but also putting them on the map. Yet, in a matter of weeks or months of an episode's air date, that newly lauded establishment stood the risk of becoming a shell of its former self: the dreaded and rightly maligned tourist trap. Bourdain was decidedly not in the business of transmuting hole-in-the-wall gems into fanboy fodder, as he explained on NPR's *Fresh Air* in 2016. Gastronomy aficionados would have to make pilgrimages following the spirit of his travel law rather than the letter.

What's any of this got to do with sunglasses? Eye protection and chic accessories aside, behind his Persols, Bourdain preserved a modicum of his inner world. It's the slightest visual cue that while he is literally broadcasting his international itinerary for our entertainment, he's still keeping some of it to himself. Make no mistake, it's a curated life—we're seeing only what he wants us to see.

For those who partake in social media's glossy, filtered charms, it's difficult to gauge exactly where documenting one's life ends and brazen performativity begins. Which is why it's so remarkable that in 2021, three years after his death, *Rolling Stone* uncovered an anonymous Reddit account* Bourdain created to write about Brazilian jiu-jitsu, his late-in-life passion. The hallmarks of his inimitable voice are all there under the username NooYawkCity. Through roughly 80 posts spanning three years, he shares his inner musings, triumphs and failures with a community of like-minded martial arts enthusiasts. One imagines it was a source of comfort for a man who lived the last two decades of his life for the world to see. For anyone left reeling in the wake of his demise, it's a reassurance that his unedited, unvarnished self was just as bold, thoughtful and honest as what you got on TV.

Take a note from Bourdain: There's joy to be found in keeping a few things to yourself rather than exploiting them for views or money. Don't lose your soul in the rush to secure likes, followers and fortune.

---

*His widow, Ottavia Busia-Bourdain, and a source close to Bourdain confirmed to *Rolling Stone* that it was his account.

Parts Unknown,
"Las Vegas" (S3E2).

> "Early moralists who believed that taking too much pleasure at the table led inexorably to bad character—or worse, to sex—were (in the best-case scenario, anyway) absolutely right."
>
> —*The Nasty Bits*

Who's afraid of sexual excess? From cornflakes to graham crackers to granola, many bland light bites got their start because Victorian vegetarians waged a crusade on flavor as a means of containing *other* appetites.

As Bourdain points out in the quote above, reformers knew deep in their bones that indulging in a toothsome dish would surely lead the faithful astray (and those Protestant eugenicists certainly couldn't have that).

Unless you're an ascetic or a masochist,* there's little point in denying yourself. Next time you graze off a charcuterie board, remember: Reject the morality police one bite at a time.

---

*Not that there's much difference.

"Naturally,
I'm misanthropic.
But the Negronis are
helping considerably."
—*The Nasty Bits*

LAUGH INTO THE VOID

NO MATTER WHAT bizarre, dangerous or utterly absurd situation Bourdain found himself in, he could always be counted on to provide a well-timed pithy remark. This was not a random characteristic he happened to acquire over the course of his travels or switched on only while the cameras were rolling but a signature facet of his overall approach to life. When the squid aren't biting on the fishing trip, the local fixer is a bullshit artist and nothing's going as expected, there's something to be said for meeting what comes your way with a joke up your sleeve.

There's no denying that food tells a story.
But feasts aside, what Bourdain seemed
especially hungry for was a chance
to forge a genuine connection with
the people he encountered.
At their best, meals are a tasty conduit for
sampling the best of what humanity has to offer:
our shared stories of oppression,
conquest, liberation and triumph over the odds.
But you'll never savor that level of
inner richness if you can't bring yourself to
ask someone what's on their mind.

On the 86th-floor observatory to
light the Empire State Building orange
(the color of hunger awareness)
in recognition of the Food Bank for
New York City on November 1, 2011.

"I'm a restless person....
I recognized early on
I'm not a guy who
should have a lot
of time to contemplate
the mysteries of
the universe.
I need to stay busy.
I need to have
a project to schedule.
That's just the nature
of my demons."

—*GQ*, January 18, 2017

KEEP MOVING

SAY YOU'VE HIT the big time. Got your name in the paper for demonstrating considerable skill, charm and wit. Dream job under your belt, bank account in the black and ripening nicely. Perhaps you've had a chance to make sound investments, marry someone whose company you crave, find a place to call your own and fill it with curated objects that bring you joy. Maybe you've welcomed a child, manifesting your ascent into the pantheon of parenthood. So...what else is left to accomplish, beyond waking up every day? Scarfing down your three square meals, putting in your hours, then straight to bed to do it all over again. What boxes remain unchecked? What then?

If this nightmare thought scenario preyed on Anthony Bourdain's mind, his saving grace came in 2014 in the form of a swift kick to the shin: Brazilian jiu-jitsu. At the time, his wife, Ottavia, had introduced him to mixed martial arts training, having first caught the bug in 2008. A few short years into watching his wife mold her body into a force to be reckoned with, by the time he first stumbled out of the ring, he'd found his new high. Except this high prompted him to quit smoking and get fit. This newest Bourdain—the gray-haired ass-kicking machine—even took home a gold medal at the International Brazilian Jiu-Jitsu Federation's New York Spring International Open Championship in 2016. No small feat for a 59-year-old newcomer to the sport with a demanding day job working for one of the most famous news networks in the world.

But in that surprising, punch-in-the-gut way that real life trumps fiction, Bourdain's literary career ended with help from the friend who saw it take wing. Novelist Joel Rose bookended Bourdain's long arc from chef who wrote in the off-hours to author to TV host, author and jiujiteiro. The same storyteller who created the indie mag *Between C & D*—and who recognized Bourdain's unique voice as early as the 1980s—co-wrote Bourdain's final literary project, the posthumously released graphic novel *Hungry Ghosts*, which features eight hair-raising tales told by a team of chefs looking to scare the shit out of each other while catering the dinner party of a Russian oligarch. It boasts a *Tales from the Crypt*-style framework, wherein a nameless, evil shape-shifting spirit takes a seat among the unfortunate dinner guests and introduces the stories that follow: tales of lust, greed, gluttony, indiscretion and a host of other sins, all strung together through the unifying thread of food. This shapeshifter, who has a sinister plan in place for the guests, is in some ways a stand-in for Bourdain, the "hungriest ghost," as Rose calls him in the novel's acknowledgments. Bourdain's projects are too numerous, his passions and contributions too varied to list, but *Hungry Ghosts* makes for one hell of a send-off. Bourdain packed more into 61 years than most do in 100.

Perhaps that's the overarching lesson of Bourdain's life and career, rather than the laundry list of dining do's and don'ts outlined to pragmatic perfection in *Kitchen Confidential*: If you've got the spark, the drive and the time, you can reinvent yourself as many times as you'd like.

Parts Unknown,
"Bahia, Brazil" (S3E8).

> "Open your mind, get up off the couch, move."
>
> —*No Reservations,* "Brooklyn" (S9E10)

"If I do have any advice for anybody," Bourdain says in the *No Reservations* finale (S9E10), "any final thought, if I'm an advocate for anything, it's to move as far as you can, as much as you can, across the ocean or simply across the river." Like a grizzled, tattooed Atticus Finch, Bourdain signs off his Travel Channel series by reminding us how important it is to crawl around in someone else's skin. It's a big world. You heard the man: What are you waiting for?

"I should've died in my 20s. I became successful in my 40s. I became a dad in my 50s. I feel like I've stolen a car—a really nice car—and I keep looking in the rearview mirror for flashing lights. But there's been nothing yet."

—*Biography.com*, 2016

DRIVE IT LIKE
YOU STOLE IT

T'S IMPOSSIBLE TO look at the stunning trajectory of Anthony Bourdain's career without engaging in the macabre game of wondering where it all went wrong in his youth (not including that first oyster, of course). His childhood reads like a post-war American pastoral: Middle-class Jersey boy born to married parents, complete with family vacations in France, an early exposure to the arts, a little brother with whom he was close—what's not to like? Much, apparently. The way Bourdain saw it, as he told *The Guardian* in 2013, he'd been born too late to take part in the acid-laced counterculture of the 1960s, so he spent the rest of his youth angry about it. By the time he dabbled in drugs as a teenager, he might as well have been making up for lost time. At 24, he consummated his relationship with addiction by shooting up heroin. Cocaine soon followed. Like with all volatile pairings, rock bottom wasn't far behind: At his worst, he would pick paint chips out of his carpet, smoking them in hopes they were crack pebbles. Ultimately, vanity pushed him to get clean—"I didn't like what I saw in the mirror," he confessed to *The New Yorker* in 2017. But Bourdain's dance with drugs colored the way he viewed the rest of his life.

You'd be hard-pressed to read the chef's reflection on what he made of his life's second act and not hear the whisper of impostor syndrome. For everything he accomplished and overcame, for all the years he vanquished inner demons and chemical dependencies to go on and receive critical, worldwide acclaim, Bourdain wore no rose-colored glasses. No amount of success could sway him from the feeling that, decades of tenacity and endurance aside, it could all disappear just as suddenly as it came.

When you're saddled with doubt—that irksome know-it-all that never shuts up—there's something to be said for pressing on in spite of that awful feeling. Never taking a gig for granted, always scanning the horizon in search of new opportunities, allowing yourself to be consumed by that hunger most often found in young people or anyone dragged by a cruel turn of fate into desperate means—these are potent antidotes to self-pity, excess and lethargy.

One wonders if Bourdain ever learned to like what he saw in the mirror.

If you can't manage to bludgeon your inner critic into submission, Bourdain's career might just stand as evidence that you can at least trick yourself into thinking you're pulling a long con. Better still, you might get away with it. Just don't get caught up looking in the rearview mirror. If you count yourself among the late-bloomers or second-chancers, if living a life you're proud of feels like you've hopped behind the wheel of someone's midlife crisis for a joyride of indeterminate length, floor it.

ACKNOWLEDGMENTS

Thank you to Jeff Ashworth, Tim Baker, Susan Dazzo, Noreen Henson, Madeline Raynor, Phil Sexton, Tara Sherman, Dave Weiss and the rest of the incredible team at Topix Media Lab for your unrelenting talent, generosity and patience. I continue to learn so much from you all.

I'd also like to thank my parents for giving me the opportunity to travel abroad as a 22-year-old (coincidentally, the age Bourdain recommended in *Medium Raw*) at a difficult moment in my life when I needed it most.

My deepest gratitude to my husband. Thank you, my love, for being my greatest supporter as we continue this journey together.

JULIANA SHARAF is a longtime fan of Anthony Bourdain and the author of *Everything I Need to Know I Learned from Betty White, Everything I Need to Know I Learned from Dolly Parton, What Would Harry Do?* and more. When she isn't penning or editing books for Media Lab Books, she enjoys mainlining espresso and savoring the spoils of the greater Miami food scene. She and her husband live in Florida with their dog, Brisket, and their daughter, who was born during the production of this book.

Media Lab Books
For inquiries, contact customerservice@topixmedia.com

ISBN-13: 978-1-956403-72-5
ISBN-10: 1-956403-72-8